A Gift and a Curse

A Gift and a Curse

Author: Sinead McGuigan

Instagram: @sineadmcgpoetry

Cover art: Sébastien Meyrignac

Instagram: @blackliquidink

A Gift and a Curse

Copyright © 2021 Sinead McGuigan

All rights reserved.

ISBN: 9798713787608
Imprint: Independently published

A Gift and a Curse

Dedicated to Kathleen, my mother.

Wander in my maze of thoughts...

Contents

1. A Gift and a Curse
2. Dawn
3. The Divinity of Truth
4. Blinded
5. Tapestry of Life
6. Imagine Wild
7. Bloom
8. Shades of me
9. The Edge of a Dream
10. Twilight Thoughts
11. Whispers in the Wind
12. A Fallen Angel
13. Red Petals
14. A New World
15. River Eyes
16. Only Us

17. Requiem

18. Cancer

19. Passing

20. Garlands

21. Pools

22. The Shore of Life

23. The Burden of My Love

24. Angel's Wings

25. Immortal Love

26. Eternal Bliss

27. Winter

28. Dark Angel

29. Tides of Longing

30. Black Soil

31. Love's Dream

32. Repentance

33. Lost Moments

34. Beloved

35. Kaleidoscope

36. Darkness

37. I Saw a Bird Fly Backwards

38. Weightless

39. Empty Space

40. Broken Wings

41. Painting Dreams

42. This Precious Life

43. Searching

44. Cosmic Love

45. Rose's

46. Rebirth

47. Solace

48. Utopian Dreams

49. Butterfly Wings

50. Awakening

51. Solitude

52. The Forest of Forgetting

53. Eternal Love

54. Invisible Moons

55. Vines

56. Shrinking Windows

57. She is Love

58. Us

59. Holy Wine

60. Snake

61. Beloved Dead Body

62. Reflection

63. Kiss the Sun

64. End

65. The Edge of Reason

66. Spinning

67. A Quiet Place

68. Dream into Me

69. Frozen Memories

70. Poetic Dreams

A Gift and a Curse

A Gift and a Curse

In the absence of sun

I am shapes of light

breathing my gift

into your mouth

I am an ocean of love

streaming into your heart

caressing you

in waves of longing

I am hidden in tides

that long to hold you

rising in blissful rapture

sweeping you away

I am stillness held

in the quiet depths

A Gift and a Curse

pressing my lips

against the chaos

I am shadows dancing

in foaming waters

crashing ashore

in exhilaration

I am the ocean spray

droplets of love

kissing your lips

with my salty tears

I am a gift and a curse

caught in the breeze

thirsting for you

in an ocean of poetry

Dawn

For what are dreams without eyes

to look upon melancholic fields of truth?

They plunder my feverish plight,

sanctify my most chaste body strewn,

break the silence of dagger tears as

gentle breezes dance upon the blades.

Awakened by soft mountain dew,

transparent memories nourish parched lips.

Darkened thoughts stretch to bloom,

sun reflections dazzle in the midst of change—

Hollow sight blossoms to fertile springs,

I open my eyes to the dawning day

The Divinity of Truth

Beneath the bending glass

knowing hands submerge me

in solemn prayer I descend

into the divinity of buried truth

holy bells echo in the depths

rippling atonement

reflections gasping

pull on watery ropes

ringing in sounds of holy bliss

lucid thoughts drown in nostalgic longing

drifting off into pools of contemplation

my eyes brimming with tears

cry for mercy

A Gift and a Curse

my body is spirited by eternal floods

into a peaceful eternity

as those knowing hands hold me

in the purity of light

I rest in the divinity of peace

Blinded

There are no eyes

behind the blindfold

of the unfree

the unseeing of reality

no dreams to bleed

no smiling lips

behind masked mouths

drinking in drops

of toxic misery

There are no ears

filled with blood

echoing in time

no imagination

sparking minds eye

A Gift and a Curse

A golden fleece

laid across dreams

jewels glitter false visions

until their shine dies

There are no bodies

wrapped in silver threads

escaping labyrinths

of the undead

There are no hands

holding ropes

half human hearts

tongues licking stones

in medusa's clutch

A Gift and a Curse

There are no eyes

behind the blindfold

of the unfree

the unseeing of reality

no dreams to bleed

A Tapestry of Life

In silken sheets of tragedy

she met her sad demise

perished her humanity

curtains draw on

luminosity of life

her mind once a tapestry

of unconscious pure delight

now fragmented

broken thoughts

hang in dark blackout blinds

her body once embroidered

carved in scared ancient art

chords tighten on gaping wounds

as vibrancy departs

A Gift and a Curse

her heart once mirrored

stories of love and devotion

sacred gold hieroglyphics

etched,

tarnished with emotions

melancholic sobs fill her veins

chilled blood of regret

 her existence denied

dreams to vivid

crying from her breast

she breathes in her last

death gnawing on her bones

tearing flesh from limbs

scars weaved in bloody tones

A Gift and a Curse

in the silken sheets of tragedy

where immortality begins

unbidden

she rises

laced in crimson sins

Imagine Wild

Imagine you are waking

in the sigh of a breath

lost between lips

mouthing dreams

do you feel the blow

of distracted thoughts

biting down hard

grinding regret

palms holding your cries

for licking tongues

drowning in fantasy

scars smiling wide

A Gift and a Curse

inviting dream lids

to fill the space

under closed eyes

imagine wild

imagine ears snigger

in disbelief

applauding sheets

the silence you seek

their purpose obscure

a faded down

dreams languishing

coloured gems of mist

imagine sliding down

transparent slides

A Gift and a Curse

archaic temples

of silver and gold

seeking silent visions

a leaning dawn

in the sleeping sigh

of a waking breath

the beauty of an eye

mirrors blazing dreams

cracked wanton whispers

mouthing dreams

half breathed regrets

longing sighs

Imagine you are waking

in the sigh of a breath

Bloom

When the first bloom of love called us

how we danced among the leaves

rose's opening to full hearts

vibrant red on scarlet cheeks

a gust of wind flew through our love

scattered us wide and far apart

entangled us in wildest roots

dusted brown on pale sad face

from the trees will you come back to me

when petals drop from their buds

will your heart once again be mine

withered trees stoop in colder clime

A Gift and a Curse

When rains pour down on loves trust

we no longer dance among the leaves

I'm a droplet clinging to blooms of love

floating petals in streams of tears

Shades of Me

I bury myself in poetry

elaborate shades of me

stripped bare

merged with nature

my true love

wrapped in fantasy

I cut lines into the earth

I write deep parts in time

I caress the soil with empty hands

finding beauty

designing rhymes

A Gift and a Curse

shapes of sounds

echo deep

words weave kissing lips

transparent in the night

silent breaths longingly drift

eyes wide at such a sight

the gentle breeze

touches my tongue

whispering poems

humming clouds

open mouths

crying in soft tones

A Gift and a Curse

I am peaceful in this versed soil

dirt clinging to my bones

my poetic heart beats and dreams

to the dark spirit of my muse

I write to you

to explore our truth

to feel our love

fill mystic layers

I submerge myself in your being

wandering forever in

our poetic dreams

The Edge of a Dream

I sleep on the edge of a dream

a forest reflective of who I might be

I imagine myself exist in a language

(of trees)

silent winds hug trembling branches

night advances

as they gently caress me

I exist in the darkness

vague shapes emerge

(plead)

a solitary existence

hidden in leaves

A Gift and a Curse

My spirit transcends

binding my flesh

(to the earth)

I am running deeper

(returning)

my reflection inhales dirt

I am tired of the day

I am lost in the night

I am in a forest of

wandering bones

where roots running deep

try to decipher me

I sleep on the edge of a dream

Can you find me?

Twilight Thoughts

Writing in twilight of summer days

under shades of glossy trees

her eyes hold secrets of her heart

bittersweet scent in the breeze

She writes of winters apprehensive chill

of icy lakes and crystal paths

lips of blue impart their plea

shaped beneath the shiny glass

Between the kisses of the wind

cool frozen eyes endure the gale

deep caverns hold running streams

mouthing eloquent words outcast

A Gift and a Curse

Love flurries as winter breaks

the winter sun regretfully sighs

spring blooms, a restless heart awake

charming sounds of morning cries

Writing in the summer heat

a flaming passionate sunrise glow

dazzled by the blaze of light

waiting for the autumn blow

Her eyes hold secrets of her heart

lashes rain in falling leaves

Fill the seasons with her love

sweet dreams of us ever grieves

Whispers in the Wind

When you feel death

longing for your earthly remains

embalming your skin with a holy scent

ancestral whispers caught in the wind

scatter upon you as withered flowers

Yet you breathe

Death caressing your soul in delight

enticing you into poured blessings

wetting your lips with holy water

Yet you breathe

A Gift and a Curse

When you feel death

shudder in anticipation

at the threshold of existence

The solitude of a lonely grave

pulling you into the sunken dark

engulfing you in grief

Yet you breathe

Syncopated energies

capture your eyes

spinning into unfathomable depths

until you slip beyond the pain

Breathe

Stay awhile under the heat of the sun

feel its warmth on your chilling bones

languish in sensations of connection

mesmerised by sensual undertones

Inhale magical moments of life

intricate mysteries hidden untold

you are not ready to leave

you want to stay

feel the earth

beneath your feet

you are alive

fate holds your story

tears hold your secrets

you are still here

Breathe

Fallen Angel

A fallen angel, you came to me

cradled me in open arms.

Buried yourself in my beauty,

away from the burning sun.

We rise and fall in the night,

embrace in enchanted skies.

Wings of passion pull us close,

lost under the trembling moon.

I see your darkness, you see mine.

as we fly in the dark liquid sky.

Red Petals

I see beauty in darkness

mysteries untold

I weave garlands of flowers

keep me warm from the cold

I see skies of blue wrapped

around darkest thoughts

I paint trails of red petals

embroider silk cloths

cloaking my skin

from the burning sun

hanging a veil

weave inside skies undone

to shelter my eyes

red petals held tight

emotions evolve as

night turns to light

I see light in darkness

a journey divine

paths of gold shimmer

I travel through time

I see warm hues in clouds

scattered fractions of thoughts

that glitter and point

beyond the stars in the north

A Gift and a Curse

raining softly, fragrant petals red

creation hanging on silver threads

I see beauty through dark pupils

eyes burning bright

visions, optical illusions

thoughts inspire sight

shining through rainbows

vibrant colourful hues

I see artistry raining

sweet petals of truth

I see connection

glowing in prismatic light

A Gift and a Curse

I see shadows fade

into dark tinted night

I see delicate crystals

frosted in time

I see love reflecting

how my eyes shine

I see promises

scatter across my eyes

I see beauty in darkness

red petals of lives

A New World

Deep in the glassy lake of despair

humanity was strewn in a deep void

searching for reflections of exquisite

colours, pounding with a relentless faith

crystalline beauty now icy grinds

cracked images into frozen visions

shivering indifference made us blind

to the natural beauty of our time

In the awakening of a new world

as the sun converses with the moon

A Gift and a Curse

A new understanding begins to dawn

penetrating the dark opaque gloom

touching cosmic stars of grief

melting visions start to stream

From chaos unwinding trails illumine

a regeneration of spiritual belief

Crimson fragments regroup and shine

in the constellations of diversity

Humanity basks in sunlit days

a new naked truth for eternity

River Eyes

There is a river in her eyes

frayed at the edges

drowning a procession of sounds

straining irises to write on lenses

clearing the debris of doubt from her mind

her body is hollowed by tides of thoughts

stammering words into existence

wading deeper into depths of her

to scatter on banks with teeming pleas

how cold the sound of chattering silence

that lashed her past with draining dread

her future releases impetus floods

colliding dreams of truth unsaid

A Gift and a Curse

there is a river in her eyes

brimming with poetry

rendering wisdom

touching in serendipity

Only Us

I close my eyes

to the darkness

There is you

only you

cast in shadows

sunlight dimmed

breathing against the dawn

There is you

half hidden

longing to stay

A Gift and a Curse

in the tenderness of my eyes

drowning in dreams of us

only you

Dance in my tears

in the fluidity of my love

where the essence of self

floats in pools of freedom

bringing you deeply into day

There is only you

thirsty and hungry

merciless in love

I wait for you

A Gift and a Curse

I draw you close

under an enchanted sky

Light fades

beating hearts

pulse in the galaxies

There is only you

There is only me

fused in the darkness

breathing against the night

There is only love

only u

Requiem

Finger the soil

filled with remains

wreaths hiding

the stench of death

open and bloom

Fluids once stagnant

in the shallows

stream and flow

cleansing all sin

held in the undertow

Requiem sounds

fill hollow spaces

notes penetrate wood

arousing spirits

A Gift and a Curse

Past betrayal forgotten

spirits absorbing light

unconscious thoughts

hope slowly ignites

Kiss the humble earth

hands clasped in prayer

in the absence of anger

humanity grieves

In a dreamless state

moments of life stir

the soul bound

to the elements

awakens once more

A Gift and a Curse

Finger the soil

filled with remains

death has no air

no grave to hold

Cancer

Questions I ponder

I live or die

It all hangs in the shadows

Will flowers open their buds to the sun

or close to protect their petals from the rain?

Will the cuckoo's song sing in May

or the tides come and go each day?

Will clouds cling to moist darkened sky

or the rain fall to earth with cleansing sighs?

We live or die

It all hangs in the shadows

A Gift and a Curse

Will we awaken each morning to the sunrise?

Will earth keep spinning emotional tides?

Will gravity pull us towards the moon

or astronauts stay afloat or marooned ?

Will the oceans rage against the storm

or turbulent waves fight against the norm?

My being is suspended in static state

vines tighten around my furious fate

Let me sink into the dark abyss

touch the lips of deaths longing kiss

My forlorn body is tired and still

But yet I cling (I cling)

I do not fall

I cling

Passing

Eternal breathes hold jagged silence

pleading for tempestuous ties

probing kisses watched by eyes of languor

fill skies with clustered mouths

we danced in the centre of me

under eternal springs of alchemy

shadows suckle under the veil of night

reflections bending iridescent beams

Unexpected

floating in the Dead Sea

kissing forbidden parts of me

A Gift and a Curse

caressing the crush of a new existence

scattered in poetic dreams

spirits pour sharp blades of thought

into forests of lotus eaters

Unbodied

we danced into sleeping valleys

digging gravity into the roots of time

we moved our minds in fluidity

immersed in dark clouded skies

Passing

Garlands

At one with nature here I lie

divine murmurs caress my tongue

my tears cast soothing streams of calm

springs of connection gaining trust

the earth trembles with ritualistic dreams

the sun holds my form in light

flames of passion whisper in the wind

the moon protects my tender heart

loves pleasure seek fragrant leaves

precious garlands of dark surrounding me

A Gift and a Curse

my love for you is planted deep

in pagan soil where true hearts bleed

majestic rivers chant heavenly sounds

rapids surge and swell in waves

smothering the flames of despair

dreams of us shrouded by the night

alas my love if you could only see

how the stars shine bright liberating me

my light spirals in your dreamless rays

awaken enchantment in your days

lying together in wondrous nights

your despair in ashes gasp at the sight

A Gift and a Curse

for love can take us beyond our dreams

rapturous moments within the leaves

Pools

On the surface of indifference

I do not drown

you cannot extract my shutting eyes

from the calm of immortal wings

flying in utopian dreams

free floating tongues

whisper through deep waters

surrounding my body's outline

the fluency of sound

not lost in translation

A Gift and a Curse

ripples sigh morality in continuous flow

pecking the compassion from my lips

I feel consciousness lie between

darkness and light

preserving death by living

in a sea of transparency

a deeper pool

I exist

The Shore of Life

At the edge of dusk

lamenting paths

dying from exposure

to eternal rain

flood with emerging

memories

held too long

under the surface

of existence

empty words

of a drowning mind

swim in pools

of emotional pain

A Gift and a Curse

emerging

into storming waves

against the quiet

merging with the rain

washing away

perpetual darkness

scattering new drops of

acceptance

on the ever changing

shore of life

The Burden of my Love

Maybe it was too much to bare

the burden of my love

It a rare complexity burning crucibles of passion

transcending beyond this world

A sensual longing, to understand the aspirations of a provocative mind

A deeper spiritual connection

abandoning all constraints, free to spill emotional blood into the earth's core

Lie naked in creative imagination creating mystical rings of fantasy

Dragging each other dazed through hurricanes,

our sweet fascination ripe with aspirations, now blown asunder

Dreams outstretching drapes of conformity lost in silent nights

I worshiped you

your artistic precious truth coloured my soul

A Gift and a Curse

My tears fall, but do not flow

as I lock them in caskets beneath my slowly freezing heart

Oh how I long for the caress of your words

where crystals now tear my skin

Shall we find our temple,

lie upon the altar ?

Be as one

to conquer my anguished heart?

Angel's Wings

Every day I wrap my spirit around you

foat within the essence of your being

 as your heart beats I fill your veins with love

as you breathe in I give you all my strength

I gently cleanse your face with my tears

your eyes water as I kiss your lids

my hand never leaving the touch of you

moving slowly over your tired limbs

caressing your weary body until you feel warm

surrender to my embrace

A Gift and a Curse

my love fills you with an energy

surrounding you in heat

I am with you to keep you safe

to ease your burden

feel our connection burning

erasing the darkness

so I can bask in the knowledge of you

and one day touch your beautiful face

and smile towards the sun

as we walk towards the ocean

hands entwined

knowing

A Gift and a Curse

there is only us

under the shadow

of angels wings

Immortal Love

I am invisible

yet you see me

dipping your pen

into my eyes of longing

slowly you etch beautiful

text upon my skin

ink me in potent lines

create a story

journey in me

how can you see the map of me?

within your eyes I am perfection

yet my flaws are held

steadfast in another's hold

A Gift and a Curse

in silent nights there is only you

whispering your name

I shade my eyes from

the morning sun

lingering in moments of us

tracing the contours of our fusion

only under the moon can

our immortal love shines

in constant turmoil

I must endure the day

as sunlight penetrates my lids

my heart cries for you

until the shadow of your hand

reaches for me in the darkness

carrying me to places unknown

Eternal Bliss

I am the subtle touch within a breeze

the gentlest kiss on tender lips

hum melodious notes on sensual ear

the sounds of truth within your eyes

I am the vision of silence in the snow

the coldest kiss on icy lips

the pale cheeks chilled with grief

shivering body in still air

I am the deepest blush of the sun

the hottest kiss on passionate lips

murmurs ignite wondrous sight

bright eyes burning through life's shade

A Gift and a Curse

I am the tranquil sounds across the sky

the sweetest kiss on eager lips

eyes thirsting visionary joy

ripple in celestial air

I am the darkest eclipse of the moon

the everlasting kiss on blessed lips

enraptured in my love for you

eyes penetrating eternal bliss

Winter

I want to live in eternal winter,

to feel the cool chill on my bones.

Lie in the frozen ground,

my heart icy unfeeling, still.

I want the snow to drift upon me,

bury me deep out of sight.

Love brought me here

into the cold eternal night.

My dying eyes hold unshed tears,

filled with sorrow, crying tears of black.

A Gift and a Curse

Perished with the cold,cracked in despair,

the frozen earth binds me with loving care.

Wrapped in a shroud,winter holds me.

Numb body surrenders,your cruel intent.

The winter sun shines,through the hailstorm

thawing the chill,of your biting lament.

Love brought me here, to rival death.

Love left me here, I draw my last breath.

Dark Angel

I am a dark angel

reaching towards you

with blinding light

I am sorrowful tears

drowning you in memories

of a beautiful world

I am haunting pain

caressing you

in divine healing

I am darkness breaking

transparent barriers

with soft breathes

A Gift and a Curse

I am remorse

lying beside you

dissolving your distress

I am fire

feeding fiery thirst

embracing your grief with warmth

I am death

buried in the earth

smothering you with kisses of life

My eyes are closed to the darkness

Flooded with visions of life

I am darkness

bringing you light

Tides of Longing

My tears are pools of longing

deepest ocean blue

lost moments drowning

in elements of you

reaching for your hand

now distant and cold

lost moments drowning

trickle away into the sands

My tears hold you oh so tight

as currents tie you down

lost moments weep for us

silently tossing pain around

visions of our intimate love

ripple in the tide

shimmers of our memories

arouse sensations deep inside

My tears fall upon your skin

passions stream us towards a kiss

greedily you drink me in

heated caresses ever missed

memories of us are whispered

across the ocean floor

in your arms I die again

tides casting me to shore

A Gift and a Curse

My tears are pools of longing

weeping for our mortal love

restless sleep implores you

as waves crash from above

death has left me dreams of us

living under lids of blue

Currents swell taking me

forever away from you

Black Soil

I feel the pain it's tearing me

ripping through my skin

gnawing at my organs

causing such a din

I've lost all reason

to live or to die

I'd rather feel this suffering

than nothing left inside

It's the nonchalance

that kills me

searing in my veins

A Gift and a Curse

The nothingness of nothing

escaping once again

bleeding out at force

flowing through the earth

It's the only place to comfort me

this lost forgotten place

the blackened soil warms me

encapsulates my soul

to return to the ground

be still my only goal

I feel no more pain

as petals shroud my plight

A Gift and a Curse

my screams silent desolate

sorrows nourished hold tight

I embrace the ever quiet

in darkness now I lie

It is this feeling that heals me

when I don't want to die

Love's Dream

I am hidden in sweet sorrow

a pure and lonely place

eyes shrouded by petals

I hide from death's embrace

I hide myself in secrets weaved

in crushed velvet threads

at night I lie lamenting laid

out in flowering beds

At dawn I descend

I lie beside your bones

corpses comfort my limbs

I'm no longer lost alone

A Gift and a Curse

Dreams of golden eternity

shine from these damned souls

the scent of remembrance

withering in soft tones

Our love, our bleeding hearts

still stemming from my eyes

I am hidden in sadness

where loves dream never dies

Repentance

At graves edge flowers wither

gaunt faces kneel in silent prayer

black petals strain with crystal vows

memories ache in crusted teardrops

as dark shadows caress the lens

taking absolution from pious drops

thorns cut deep into mortal hearts

dissolve sins in scattered ash

dark creatures incensed by hymns

helplessly dance on cracking bones

spread their wings as thorns blaze

scorched stories light darkened skies

shallow graves breath flowers scent

ripples of humanity long repent

Lost Moments

As I lie in the foliage

dying in your arms

your tears fall upon me

crying in alarm

cradled in your hold

my last breath is near

longing to save me

with each falling tear

alas my love

my time has come

to go underground

where life's story sung

remains whisper notes

silent in their sound

the air is so still

your tears fall to ground

entangle my body

in dark roots of me

twisted mangled weeds

slowly start to feed

Taking their fill

holding limbs fast

your tears absorbed

left shaken aghast

A Gift and a Curse

embedded into soil

dragging me down

your pleas unanswered

in endless earths coil

smothered eternal

I'm falling so deep

slipping from your hold

your strong hands retreat

leaves fall from the trees

as body grows cold

open hands closing tight

emptiness unfolds

A Gift and a Curse

It's all eerie now

a stillness descends

the rustle of the leaves

as memories now blend

my eyes are wide

as crimson tears flow

for lost moments of us

that we will never know

Beloved

Lay me on papyrus pillow

between silk sheets of poetry

resting on prose and tragedy

drenched in beauty and grace

hold me with precious texts

bequeathed by ancient scrolls

arouse enshrined thoughts

with sense of possibility

lines mystical in nature

evoke lyrical moments

as you infuse my form

with the vibration of poetry

Kaleidoscope

I'm lost in the abyss of your love

I'm drowning it its intricate patterns of us

The shadow you tattoo on my gaping skin

bleeds for you in its stunning scene

Lose yourself in provocative me

In the contours of my linguistic grace

Can't you feel me? I offer myself to you

in the meandering shadows of my imagination

Take me, I am yours to explore

plunge into my alluring vision

I die now as I wait

A Gift and a Curse

mindless in your mind, It's beyond the realms

Can't you see fiery eyes aflame?

inhale my scent of sweetest flower's and smouldering fires

touch my essence with waves of splendour

You are haunted by my taste as we bath in steaming surrender

nothing can change our fate

We are one, radiant lovers of endless want

caressing our wildest desires in rapture with such delicate intimacy

raging passion immersed in sanguine colours collide like cherry bombs

hot kisses on lips explode unknown pleasures

thrills scream with cries of exquisite moans

A Gift and a Curse

bewildered fervent bodies banish reality

free to savour loves taste in seductive mind

languish deep inside my fantasy

A kaleidoscope of sensations

intoxicating waves of impulsive longing

I am yours

Darkness

I wanted to hide underground

to let the black soil fill my mouth

feel my nostrils fill with dirt

blind my eyes with dark relief

My last breath exhaled your name

lips pressed together holding grief

whispering memories into lonely thoughts

You, the sun radiated my warmth

I, the glimmer of light in your dark

I, the moon that shone with golden vision

You, the love that grieves for my touch

A Gift and a Curse

strangled by the loss of our love

as I fall into nothingness

shadows lighten my body

dressed in shades of promise

with speed of light

I lose my sight

visions of darkness

surround my eyes

vulnerable

scared

I reach

I long

You slip

You fall

I'm alone

I Saw a Bird Fly Backwards

I dreamed I sat beside my grave

languished in churches care

holding gracious words in mouth

out of throat came sobbing doubt

I saw a bird fly backwards

it cannot speak beak burnt red

I have no words

my tears are stone

darkened wings

across me roam

A Gift and a Curse

as I breath bittersweet life

a sinking sun blush will burn

longing eyes watch memories sleep

a ravens call my soul to keep

yesterday

I saw a bird fly backwards

finally it's gone so quiet

dreamless now condensed in time

sunlit eyes burnish death's last shine

Weightless

In your arms I rest

hold me as I fall

in a trance

weightless

humanities fate spins

into an invisible world

hold me as I fall

stars reach towards me

moonlight guides my way

the universe weaving

conscious thoughts

A Gift and a Curse

Illuminate the sky

floating

weightless

hold me as I fall

In the expansive cosmos

memories of strangers

touch me under Jupiter's gaze

rippling through the silence

engraving the sky

floating

weightless

hold me as I fall

A Gift and a Curse

distant sounds orbit me

the luminous starlight

shines in dazzling revelations

clouds brimming

with droplets of hope

shower the earth

In your arms I rest

hold me as my fall

into your infinite

universal love

Empty Space

She grew cold in an empty space

Laid bare in a heart of blooms

Where love had filled her soul with hate

blurred illusions, held in summer dews

She whispers in the silent night

to mouths of those sleepless souls

She breathes in the earthly air

petals fill their throats with moans

She hungers for those piercing thorns

to shred her vision, half blinded by trust

The moment the enchantment passed

love withered in rose leaves of dust

A Gift and a Curse

She shivers at your lost caress

stemmed naked truths through her skin

She whispers to the wind to take her

to freedom where cool mountains sing

She kissed the earth a fond farewell

Lips turn blue as lost souls embrace

She grew cold in an empty space

where roses coloured her deadly fate

Broken Wings

At the break of day

skies fill with orange hues

green trees stand tall and still

cradling birds with broken wings

chirping in their protective hold

As the sun rises with burning light

creating a gallery of wonder in our eyes

we breathe in our solemn truth

wispy clouds stop to adorn

The fragility of life imprisoned by

conscious thought

Awakens

A Gift and a Curse

gazing at the aurora

naked eyes of the soul

we breathe in our new existence

lifting the veil on humanity's strife

Look beyond the horizon

in endless wonder

birds soar

flying as angels

to a new beginning

a new life

filled with love and compassion

under a crimson sky

Painting Dreams

In an extension of her

she had invisibly brushed

the contours of his reflection

delicate strokes

holding him where fingertips meet

The time not theirs yet

palms pressed

mirroring lines of fate

In the glimpsing of a love

so rare in essence

two silhouettes painting dreams

in shades of each other

charmed against his artistic heart

A restless air

A Gift and a Curse

magnetically pulled thoughts

transcendent of this world

coloured energies blend

until she surrenders to him

in the depths of actuality

wanton upon a tossed bed

where dreams become a reality

she is love

This Precious Life

I watch death drift in the night sky

orbiting around stars

holding grievances

of my past

I exist in tears

dripping into clasped hands

whispering in ritualistic prayers

See through my eyes

filled with emptiness

invisible moons blinded by burning suns

I compel you to stare

I'm drifting in broken pieces

somewhere between dreams and reality

A Gift and a Curse

You are caught in the day

I am lost to the night

Look at my hands of grief

Look at your hands of love

Let me slip through your fingers

in blind sorrow

I exist in tears that

wash your face

as you hug this precious life

Searching

I cannot find my body

unnatural shadows gaze without sound

sweating doors swollen sigh back at them

I am asleep

I am asleep

locked in walls awake

vacant skulls

devouring eyes creep across my tender flesh

my bones surrounded by decaying faces

I am in my grave

holding my head

looking for my eyes

labouring sounds

crushed laments

Untied

lips bruised by sin and terror

disfigured walls unleaving

Mourn

I am asleep in the pane of a reflection

lost in the mind of another awake

wrestling immortal fingertips

locked in drawn shades of thought

A Gift and a Curse

thrown into these reveries

I beseech

the face of darkness

to open my eyes

searching for myself

in the void of a space

imitating me

Cosmic Love

I travel within light caught in illuminated continuum of you

Energies transpose with flickers of sound that gently caress spiritual connection

Inner parts touch without physical need

You wait as I aspire to nestle within the crux of your being

We are connected through a realm invisible to the naked eye

Our flames dance seductively creating an enhancing glow

Gases surrounding us combined are ready to combust as our desire intensifies

Anticipation suspends earth's rotation

Waves of torrent heat pulse through our bodies shocking our core

We touch as the force of the elements gravitate towards senseless excitement

Reactions heightened my voice cries your name as endless pleasures ripple in a fanatical state of ecstasy

A Gift and a Curse

Bodies expunge heat cleansing breath

Imbalanced variables sigh with relief of connection

Mesmerised our senses intoxicated by vapours spark us into the horizon

Majestic nebula smile as our union ignites eternal flames

Transcendent in nature our bodies become transformed

We are ethereal beings lost in each other

Weightless we float as burning energies through the galaxy

Exuberant moments casting cosmic tidings

We are free

We are intricate patterns within a complexity of universal illusion

Lost to the joy of reciprocity

Lost to eternal bliss of one another

A dynamic energy of existence

Lost to love

Roses

The scent of roses

the loss of love

the fading breath

in trembling leaves

the lingering sensation

the loss of life

love lost uprooted

in body of soil

the vision of beauty

the loss of sight

petals shroud eyes

in withering flowers

A Gift and a Curse

the intimate touch

the loss of hope

the longing reach

in slick sharp thorns

the quiet solitude

the loss of sound

solemn musings

in envious roots

the lingering taste

on silent lips

the scent of roses

the silent graves

mysterious buds

as all life fades

Rebirth

Embrace banquet of silent thought

behold close mouthed eloquence

divine sunflowers dance to the breeze

hushed tones whispering precious grace

glorious my moving spirit dives

into oceans of divine love

longing for an ethereal beauty

thoughts quake to thunderous notions

waves crashing flames of fiery mist

descend giving lives a new end

A Gift and a Curse

deepest dark stormy clouds

springing deaths' new beginning

each day a universal new

drizzling radiant lights beckon me

covering me in virtuous beams

I radiate in the warmth

comforted celestial souls rest

lost lives sigh forever blessed

Solace

In darkness I find solace

It's where I belong

Feel shadows of me caress your skin

My spirit inhales your mournful dreams

My kisses obliterating your fear of love

For in your darkness I feel sublime

Feel me crashing towards you now

My hands outstretched towards the bay

Longing to touch you, inhale your scent

Oh how your darkness showers over me

filling my eyes with tears of rain

A Gift and a Curse

The mystical sounds of the sea

trailing light over your tormented mind

As our human bodies in darkness sleep

our divine essence promises sight

How fragile was the lights appeal

held in your arms of watery depths

Until my darkness cradled you

shrouded you in a veil of night

The obscurity of my light speaks

every language of nightmarish dreams

A Gift and a Curse

And in the roaring of the sea

You finally touched and understood me

As you drift in a hazy sky

filled with vapours of vitality

Swirl and twirl dance and dream

fill your empty dark soul with me

My hands outstretched all alone

for our darkest souls forever roam

Utopian Dreams

Shrouded in black petals

only you can see naked waiting

for you to take me

eyes shut tight softly crying tears of red

waiting for you on my cold bed

outside I am dying chilled body strains

longing to move as slowly blood drains

inside my heart pounding cries your name

find me my love or darkness remains

souls that shriek you're near now I sense

step towards me fog clears

bodies incensed petals turn red

as you call my nameour passion is true

our fate is the flame

A Gift and a Curse

there is only you oh petals of love

embolden my skin trace every curve

your eyes devour me black petals that dream

bleed into the night red embers delight

you have placed my heart under black petals of you

I'm yours for eternity black petals of truth

Butterfly

I love how you make me feel

Inside a reality of a dream

Im fluttering my wings without a sound

I followed you in wonder through a crowd

found compassion and trust

we evolved and grew

unknown to us a longing thirst too

as a moth to a flame with lasting desire

I'm dust in your hands surrounded by power

fragrance attracts us a lingering feel

inside each other hold our dream is real

A Gift and a Curse

I love you more than you will ever know

my feelings morph expand and grow

I flapped my wings through the air you breathe

laughing embracing and planting a need

our love is freedom inhale me fast

collision of energy a spell is cast

take me as yours with most longing stare

intoxicating eyes deep pools that are rare

take me as yours our hearts merge as one

metamorphosis sheds wings burning undone

A Gift and a Curse

take me as yours such intense heat

liquids spills as our eyes meet

take me I'm yours as our blood flows

secrets thrills intense passion grows

I love how you make me feel

inside a reality of a dream

Awakening

My soul opening to the universe

inhales a mystical presence,

eyes filled with raindrops

search a distorted reality,

reflected in mirrors of time.

human suffering cries,

flooding lands

scarred by burning rage.

My tears quench the fiery flames,

filling valleys with visions of hope.

Healing waters pour through me

into the depths of my inner spirit.

A Gift and a Curse

Mountains stir at such a splendid sight,

stretching beyond the clouds in wonder.

On the dawning of a new day,

our spirits join

to soar towards the sun.

In the presence of light

fragments of humanity

laid strewn on barren land,

awaken.

Emerging

conscious from the fog,as one,

invisible currents draw us

through cleansing waters of silence.

A Gift and a Curse

Eyes blue,

the deepest oceans wide open.

Decay floats into a seabed of expectation

creating heavenly pools of reflection.

Birds sing new songs of rediscovery

My eyes behold the kaleidoscope of truth.

Solitude

I am lost to this world

Where light reflects human form

I have travelled beyond reality

into a mirage of shadows

encased in fear

dark forces hold me

my struggles are in vain

I am lost to this world

where hearts beat in human frames

blood no longer flows to vessels

stagnant pools of sanguine lie

A Gift and a Curse

vitality lost coldness instills

a savage force tears me apart

lost alone without a heart

I am lost to this world

where intimate touch triggers hope

sensations bind human hands

in synaptic connection

I'm lost to this world

tears fall as crystal droplets

shredding moments of life

frozen upon porcelain skin

haunted scenes hold me in a deep shrine

as I strain to see past the quiet

A Gift and a Curse

I am lost to this world

where angels have left me

in solitude and dark

The Forest of Forgetting

In the forest of forgetting

I run my hands along the bark

Feel the ridges scrape my hands

Hug the trunk so close to me

For inside that one

That precious tree

There is a person dear to me

Inside the trunk he crouched and hid

Serene within the falling twigs

Leaves caressed his naked skin

So soft delicate shading him

His eyes looked up towards the sky

Holding sounds of his cries

A Gift and a Curse

I wrapped myself around the tree

To show him yes you can be free

For words translated in my brain

Slowly clearing his choking throat

Easing pain from his heart

Filling hope within his veins

He felt the alone he felt the sun

A growing need to live begun

The branches weaved in magical ways

The sun it shone on memories

Burning passion for who he was

Fighting with who he feels he is

A Gift and a Curse

I dig my hands in the soil

To find that part he longs to feel

Entangled in its deepest roots

I dig and bury myself in truth

These roots hold the dearest parts of you

I gift them to you to start anew

I am the forest of forgetting

I will stay here and wait for you

I wrapped myself around the tree

The one that's precious

so dear to me

Eternal Love

In the aching night of abstraction

What was left for me to hold?

Hands now transparent

smooth crimson dreams

upon a heart that

twists and throbs

The gift of love

basking in the blooms

reaches for your longing touch

Kisses still sweet with nectar

licking delicate honey dew

A Gift and a Curse

Implore my eyes in subtlest ways

to gaze within the depths of you

Bodies arching to hungry mouths

insatiable

devour hidden parts of us

Alas centuries have passed

you are lost in the hidden earth

I cast fresh flowers upon your grave

weave garlands, under a sky of dreams

What is left for me to hold?

In the aching night of abstraction

Loss tastes insipid upon my tongue

petals wither, leaves drift to dark

Invisible Moons

I watch death drift in the night sky

orbiting around stars

holding grievances

of my past

I exist in tears

dripping into clasped hands

whispering in ritualistic prayers

See through my eyes

filled with emptiness

invisible moons

blinded by burning suns

A Gift and a Curse

I compel you to stare

I'm drifting in broken pieces

somewhere between dreams and reality

You are caught in the day

I am lost to the night

Look at my hands of grief

Look at your hands of love

Let me slip through your fingers

in blind sorrow

I exist in tears

that wash your face

as you hug this precious life

Vines

In the heart of a hill

deep vines start to grow

skies glanced down

an unexpected glow

paused for a moment

the breeze felt so warm

bringing us closer

a golden dawn

cautious amid the

escalating breeze

vines start to stretch

lovingly tease

nourished by the sun

and the gentle rain

A Gift and a Curse

embracing the warmth

two wild hearts aflame

binding together

they start to grow

beyond the clouds

to places unknown

for once it was written

across the skies

nothing could stop

their unbreakable ties

from the depths

to new heights

vines grow and grow

wrapped in awakening

entwined in two souls

A Gift and a Curse

magical mystical

aroused from afar

reaching beyond

those skies roll in awe

In the heart of a hill

under a deep blue sky

two souls lost to love

weave rapture divine

Shrinking Windows

I tell myself

I cannot write of love now

I see my grave waiting

yearning eyes hold secrets

tightly in shrinking windows

my lips pressed no longer speak

closing walls trap my dreams behind bars

I'm waiting inside the shadows of stones

packing crevices with the unknowable

cement by ears with memories of us

uttering tongues are sculptures of grief

A Gift and a Curse

my life breathes only shade

moaning mouths groan perpetually

into secret groves

all purpose lost with you

endings decay love

into tombs of death

pleasing my deaf eyes

I turn over, all for love

unmerciful

the grave devours me

elevated spirits fly

I cannot write of love now

She is Love

In an extension of her

she had invisibly brushed

the contours of his reflection

delicate strokes

holding him where fingertips meet

the time not theirs yet

palms pressed

mirroring lines of fate

in the glimpsing of a love

so rare in essence

two silhouettes painting dreams

in shades of each other

A Gift and a Curse

a restless air

charmed against

his artistic heart

magnetically pulled thoughts

transcendent of this world

coloured energies blend

until she

surrenders to him

in the depths of actuality

wanton upon a tossed bed

where dreams become a reality

she is love

Us

Your alluring charms

touched my famished spirit

A sweet enticing flavour

savoured between lips

A smile

aroused my deepest heart

Oh lover, my muse

how bitter those strange delights

held in your flesh

shatter and burst into

my delicate limbs

A touch

A Gift and a Curse

opened my deepest thoughts

teasing me in perpetual thrills

The delicate movement

of your body

A heart

heavy with the ache of love

lies within my naked breast

Listen to my soft breath

chasms of secret depths

laid bare under your gaze

A kiss

murmuring passions flow

dripping delight

into your gasping throat

A Gift and a Curse

Oh lover, my muse

how darkness surrounds me

yet entwined in your light

my eyes are nurtured

by dreams illuminated

in glimmers of hope

A look

plunged into my avid eyes

flooded with sensations

of desirous flow

engulfed in pleasure

I surrender to the

artistry of your love

Holy Wine

Time for absolution

without self deception

spilling holy wine

into drops of poetry

drink the language

get drunk on anarchy

remember written verses

of the innocent

protesting fables left their overtones

pios spirits inhabit chalices

overflowing and filled with diction

A Gift and a Curse

bow your head to the dawn of syllables

in the chanting prayers of the blessed

write to the dead and the living

Kneel

Snake

Unlock clasped hands from hissing mouths

clap as tangled vines cry out

Uncoil eyes filled with humming cones

shedding pines in silvery moss

Applauding serpents silently creep

probing venomous pools of green

Ferns exhale toxic breaths

welling in skins of leafy fronds

Gasping throats follow sinuous trails

slithering towards canopy tops

sleeping birches stretch and scatter

seeds yawn and replenish

Beloved Dead Body

Beloved dead body

how do you lie so still

strangled sounds lying mute

holding limbs unpinned

deafened by sounds

of spirits old

mouth moans stories

lost in the cold

Beloved dead body

how do you lie so still

blinded by visions

death's alluring chill

broken bones uncovered

dance in shadowy dreams

A Gift and a Curse

eyes frozen gaze through

tears that scream

Sobbing throat gasps as

bones free from skin

beloved dead body mourning

life's precious things

Petals fall black

into burnt out soil

flowers wither to dust

as darkness uncoils

Beloved dead body

all life has drifted away

Lost forlorn waiting

forever and a day

Reflection

Time to reflect

Time to regret

under burnt orange hues

I depart from my flesh

a solemn wind blows

mumbling flames

lost moments in

tangerine stone

Time to reflect

Time to regret

my bones marrowed

to a procession of prayers

A Gift and a Curse

fall from a burning cross

unending horizons

swallowed by the

bittersweet earth

Time to reflect

Kiss the Sun

Your blushing lips

kiss the sun

blinding eyes

in scarlet sin

adornments held

in throats of gods

swallow sockets

condemning love

imploding abdomens

hiding jewels

bloody wombs bleed

ritual prayers

A Gift and a Curse

love treasured

by the dead

hidden artefacts

reflecting time

open sealed eyelids

seek the divinity of light

in sunken tombs

under the blushing sun

End

I might have written endless love poems

if you had not filled my throat with lies (choking)

you etched curses on my skin

dragging me through hell (painfully)

scars twisted in winding chains

ravenous around broken limbs (grieving)

memories hugging unfinished roads

deathbeds filled with memories (withering)

strangled visions hide

in the darkness of an eye (regretting)

A Gift and a Curse

shallow verses of guilt and rage

write forgiveness to the bitter edge (healing)

dead language colours the past

no longer staining clasped hands (forgiving)

I might have written endless love poems

if you had not stabbed my heart (bleeding)

Now I write volumes

We are apart (ending)

The Edge of Reason

Silence holds tumultuous sky

sounds echo in tranquil sea

how smooth the edge of reason looks

caught in the glinting horizon

eyes rinsed by the rising sea

closed lids hold vivid dreams of us

reflections in the deepest sky

crashing into dark parts of me

engulfed by the boundless ocean

eyes pour water towards the deep

frothy veils hold a longing heart

drowning memories float away

A Gift and a Curse

I feel your truth blazing so bright

in the fiery liquid of the sun

dry my tears with your heart

feel my love from the quiet depths

Spinning

Where I find my quiet

a pinhole reflection

feeling close to the faraway

absent

freedom in the captivating

embroidered illusions

present

I am a distraction

a dusted human shape

free floating

a minute detail

creating fantasies in dreams

I move quietly

grieving senseless pain

phantoms of chaos

in a vacuum

A Gift and a Curse

sculptures of air

hug me tight

in the emptiness

spinning delight

A Quiet Place

I hold the burden of dying

bleeding in my hands

agony mocks my dying flesh

grieving

I thirst and hunger for that quiet place

for the warmth

of the soil

where the dead reside

In the chill of regrets

I linger

dirt scatters upon my weary body

shrouding me from pain

A Gift and a Curse

holy water pours light

into the barren earth

absorbing my despair

cognizance grows

I embrace the of language of rebirth

within the desperate isolation

yet somewhere in that moment

I learn to breathe

as dead wings take me

to new beginnings

where the past

is strewn in ashes

under tumultuous skies

Dream into Me

Talk to my subconscious

dream into my thoughts

lock me in a vault

keep me safe from nightmares

connection springs inspiration

fueling a complexity of ideas

Dream into me

Dream into my thoughts

reflections of reality, caught in mirrors

textures of light and dark surrounding me

shadows arched in rhythmic need

hold me in your in silent power

shine your eternal beam into my eyes

shimmering like a mirage,

blind my night terrors

fill me with vision,

A Gift and a Curse

the unseen shades of you

invade my ghostly form

my gasping spirit

be my dark angel

glistening in the distance

longing for us

an awakening of truth

open portals to the unknown

the complexity of silence

merging ideas

you dream into me

and

in the moment of silent breathes

we become one

Frozen Memories

As I lay here hidden

a world of white and blue

My frozen heart still strains

with the love I had for you

How the snow covered me

protected me from pain

But a sudden thaw

sends currents to my brain

My heart starts melting

as my body renews

The earth trembles

as blood flows anew

A Gift and a Curse

Emotions start to change

as my senses grow

a blue haze surrounds me

underneath frozen snow

My eyes have stayed closed

for centuries in the cold

Yet all I long for now is

my eyes to behold

You here with me

your love by my side

Your sensual touch

making me feel so alive

Longing for your caress

a slow warm embrace

Yet I lie here lost

A Gift and a Curse

without any trace

For the day that we wandered

up the frozen mountain side

You had already left me

wrapped

in your cold stark lies

So as my body thaws

My mind numbs it all

I lie here silent

until the next snowfall

to stay buried in a world

of white and blue

where my eyes glazed

stare eternally

at frozen memories of you

Poetic Dreams

Poetry is eloquence in silence

where I can be found.

a fragrance that surrounds me

in visible scents

how it kisses my eyes

with threads of passion

stolen moments of thought

dissolved in sheets

a rainbow of sorrows

shining in hope

A Gift and a Curse

glitters of longing

entwined in belief

how it embraces

my soul in sweet relief

poetry is fluent tongues

whispering life's moments

luscious in flavours

filled with emotion

poetry is stillness

on a watchful heart

held in secret chasms

waiting to be unravelled

A Gift and a Curse

Poetry is endless

in vision

boundless in scope

a freedom

to feel

to laugh

to love

to weep

to breathe

to explore

Poetry is insatiable hope

A Gift and a Curse

A Gift and a Curse

A Gift and a Curse

Printed in Great Britain
by Amazon